FAVORITE BRAND NAME

Easy Home Cooking

SHORTCUT
SUPPERS

Publications International, Ltd.
Favorite Brand Name Recipes at www.fbnr.com

Microwave Cooking: Microwave ovens vary in wattage. Use the cooking times as guidelines and check for doneness before adding more time.

CONTENTS

p. 46

p. 72

ALL YOU NEED IS FOUR

Seafood Risotto

■■■

1 package (5.2 ounces) rice in creamy sauce (Risotto Milanese flavor)
1 package (14 to 16 ounces) frozen fully cooked shrimp
1 box (10 ounces) BIRDS EYE® frozen Mixed Vegetables
2 teaspoons grated Parmesan cheese

• In 4-quart saucepan, prepare rice according to package directions. Add frozen shrimp and vegetables during last 10 minutes.

• Sprinkle with cheese.
Makes 4 servings

Serving Suggestion: Serve with garlic bread and a tossed green salad.

Prep Time: 5 minutes
Cook Time: 15 minutes

Easy Veggie-Topped Baked Spuds

▋▋▋

**2½ cups frozen broccoli-carrot
vegetable medley
4 large baking potatoes
1 can (10¾ ounces) cream of
broccoli soup
½ cup (2 ounces) shredded
Cheddar cheese**

1. Place vegetables in microwavable bowl. Microwave on HIGH 5 minutes; drain.

2. Scrub potatoes; pierce several times with knife. Microwave on HIGH 15 minutes or until potatoes are softened.

3. While potatoes are cooking, combine soup, vegetables and cheese in medium saucepan. Cook and stir over low heat until cheese melts and mixture is heated through.

4. Split baked potatoes in half. Top each potato with soup mixture. Add salt and pepper to taste. _Makes 4 servings_

Tip: Choose russet or Idaho potatoes for baking. Store them in a cool, dark place away from onions for up to 2 weeks. (Storing potatoes and onions together will cause the potatoes to rot more quickly.)

Prep and Cook Time:
23 minutes

Easy Veggie-Topped Baked Spuds

Hickory Smoked Ham with Maple-Mustard Sauce

Hickory chunks or chips for smoking
1 fully cooked boneless ham (about 5 pounds)
¾ cup maple syrup
¾ cup spicy brown mustard or Dijon mustard

Soak about 4 wood chunks or several handfuls of wood chips in water; drain. If using a canned ham, scrape off any gelatin. If using another type of fully cooked ham, such as a bone-in shank, trim most of the fat, leaving a ⅛-inch layer. (The thinner the fat layer, the better the glaze will adhere to the ham.)

Arrange low **KINGSFORD**® Briquets on each side of a rectangular metal or foil drip pan. Pour in hot tap water to fill pan half full. Add soaked wood (all the chunks; part of the chips) to the fire.

Oil hot grid to help prevent sticking. Place ham on grid directly above drip pan. Grill ham, on a covered grill, 20 to 30 minutes per pound, until a meat thermometer inserted in the thickest part registers 140°F.

If your grill has a thermometer, maintain a cooking temperature of about 200°F. For best flavor, cook slowly over low coals, adding a few briquets to both sides of the fire every hour, or as necessary, to maintain a constant temperature. Add more soaked hickory chips every 20 to 30 minutes.

Meanwhile, prepare Maple-Mustard Sauce by mixing maple syrup and mustard in small bowl; set aside most of the syrup mixture to serve as a sauce. Brush ham with remaining mixture several times during last 45 minutes of cooking. Let ham stand 10 minutes before slicing. Slice and serve with Maple-Mustard Sauce.

Makes 12 to 15 servings

Note: Most of the hams available today are fully cooked and need only be heated to a temperature of 140°F. If you buy a partially cooked ham, often labeled "cook before eating," it needs to be cooked to 160°F.

Note: Keep the briquet temperature low and replenish the hickory chips every 20 to 30 minutes.

Hot & Spicy Buffalo Chicken Wings

❚❚❚

1 can (15 ounces) DEL
   MONTE® Original Sloppy
   Joe Sauce
¼ cup thick and chunky salsa,
   medium
1 tablespoon red wine vinegar
   or cider vinegar
20 chicken wings (about
   4 pounds)

1. Preheat oven to 400°F.

2. Combine sloppy joe sauce, salsa and vinegar in small bowl. Remove ¼ cup sauce mixture to serve with cooked chicken wings; cover and refrigerate. Set aside remaining sauce mixture.

3. Arrange wings in single layer in large, shallow baking pan; brush wings with sauce mixture.

4. Bake chicken, uncovered, on middle rack in oven 35 minutes or until chicken is no longer pink in center, turning and brushing with remaining sauce mixture after 15 minutes. Serve with reserved ¼ cup sauce. Garnish, if desired.

Makes 4 servings

Prep Time: 5 minutes
Cook Time: 35 minutes

Lite Teriyaki Pork Chops

❚❚❚

½ cup KIKKOMAN® Lite
   Teriyaki Marinade &
   Sauce
2 tablespoons prepared
   horseradish
⅛ teaspoon ground cinnamon
4 pork rib or loin chops,
   ¾ inch thick

Blend lite teriyaki sauce, horseradish and cinnamon; pour over chops in large plastic food storage bag. Press air out of bag; close top securely. Turn bag over several times to coat all chops well. Refrigerate 1½ hours, turning bag over occasionally. Reserving marinade, remove chops. Place chops on grill 5 to 7 inches from medium-hot coals. Cook 10 to 12 minutes, or until light pink in center, turning over and brushing occasionally with reserved marinade. (Or, place chops on rack of broiler pan. Broil 5 to 7 inches from heat 8 to 10 minutes, or until light pink in center, turning over and brushing occasionally with reserved marinade.)

Makes 4 servings

Country Herb Roasted Chicken

▮▮▮

1 chicken (2½ to 3 pounds),
   cut into serving pieces
   (with or without skin) *or*
   1½ pounds boneless
   skinless chicken breast
   halves
1 envelope LIPTON® Recipe
   Secrets® Savory Herb
   with Garlic Soup Mix
2 tablespoons water
1 tablespoon olive or
   vegetable oil

Preheat oven to 375°F.

In 13×9-inch baking or
roasting pan, arrange chicken.
In small bowl, combine
remaining ingredients; brush
on chicken.

For chicken pieces, bake
uncovered 45 minutes or until
chicken is no longer pink. For
chicken breast halves, bake
uncovered 20 minutes or until
chicken is no longer pink.
                Makes about 4 servings

Menu Suggestion: Serve with a
lettuce and tomato salad,
scalloped potatoes and cooked
green beans.

Country Herb Roasted Chicken

Ravioli with Roasted Red Pepper Alfredo Sauce

▌▌▌

1 package (10 ounces) DiGIORNO® Roasted Red Bell Pepper Cream Sauce
½ cup toasted chopped walnuts
1 package (9 ounces) DiGIORNO® Four Cheese Ravioli, cooked, drained

HEAT sauce and walnuts in saucepan on medium heat.

TOSS with hot ravioli. Sprinkle with additional toasted chopped walnuts and chopped fresh parsley, if desired.

Makes 4 servings

Prep Time: 10 minutes
Cook Time: 10 minutes

Grilled Fresh Fish

▌▌▌

3 to 3½ pounds fresh tuna or catfish
¾ cup prepared HIDDEN VALLEY® Original Ranch® Salad Dressing
Chopped fresh dill
Lemon wedges (optional)

Place fish on heavy-duty foil. Cover with salad dressing. Grill over medium-hot coals until fish turns opaque and flakes easily when tested with fork, 20 to 30 minutes. Or broil fish 15 to 20 minutes. Sprinkle with dill; garnish with lemon wedges, if desired.

Makes 6 servings

Easy Veg-All® Potato Casserole

▌▌▌

1 (5.5-ounce) package au gratin potatoes
1 (15-ounce) can VEG-ALL® Mixed Vegetables, drained
1 cup cooked, cubed ham, turkey or chicken
2 tablespoons bread crumbs

Combine au gratin potatoes, vegetables and ham in medium casserole. Sprinkle with bread crumbs. Cook according to au gratin potatoes package directions. Cool 5 minutes before serving.

Makes 6 servings

Sausage Pinwheels

2 cups biscuit mix
½ cup milk
¼ cup butter or margarine, melted
1 pound BOB EVANS® Original Recipe Roll Sausage

Combine biscuit mix, milk and butter in large bowl until blended. Refrigerate 30 minutes. Divide dough into two portions. Roll out one portion on floured surface to ⅛-inch-thick rectangle, about 10×7 inches. Spread with half the sausage. Roll lengthwise into long roll. Repeat with remaining dough and sausage. Place rolls in freezer until hard enough to cut easily. Preheat oven to 400°F. Cut rolls into thin slices. Place on baking sheets. Bake 15 minutes or until golden brown. Serve hot. Refrigerate leftovers.

Makes 48 appetizers

Note: This recipe may be doubled. Refreeze after slicing. When ready to serve, thaw slices in refrigerator and bake.

Hot Sweet Potatoes

4 small (4 ounces each) sweet potatoes
2 tablespoons margarine or unsalted butter, softened
½ teaspoon TABASCO® Pepper Sauce
¼ teaspoon dried savory leaves, crushed

In large saucepan, cover potatoes with water. Cover and cook over high heat 20 to 25 minutes or until potatoes are tender. Drain potatoes and cut in half lengthwise.

Preheat broiler. In small bowl, combine margarine and TABASCO® Sauce. Spread ¾ teaspoon margarine mixture over cut side of each potato half. Season each with pinch of savory. Place on foil-lined broiler pan and broil, watching carefully, about 5 minutes or until lightly browned. Serve hot.

Makes 4 servings

Peachy Pork Roast

▮▮▮

1 (3 to 4-pound) rolled
    boneless pork loin roast
1 cup (12-ounce jar)
    SMUCKER'S® Currant
    Jelly
½ cup SMUCKER'S® Peach
    Preserves
    Fresh peach slices and
    currants for garnish, if
    desired

Insert meat thermometer into one end of roast. Bake at 325°F for 30 to 40 minutes or until browned. Turn roast and bake an additional 30 minutes to brown the bottom. Turn roast again and drain off drippings.

In saucepan over medium heat, melt currant jelly and peach preserves. Brush roast generously with sauce.

Continue baking until meat thermometer reads 160°F, about 15 minutes, basting occasionally with sauce.

Remove roast from oven. Garnish with peach slices and currants. Serve with remaining sauce.

Makes 8 to 10 servings

Note: Canned, sliced peaches can be substituted for fresh peaches.

Holiday Vegetable Bake

▮▮▮

1 package (16 ounces) frozen
    vegetable combination
1 can (10¾ ounces)
    condensed cream of
    broccoli soup
⅓ cup milk
1⅓ cups FRENCH'S® French
    Fried Onions, divided

Microwave Directions:
Combine vegetables, soup, milk and ⅔ *cup* French Fried Onions in 2-quart microwavable casserole. Microwave,* uncovered, on HIGH 10 to 12 minutes or until vegetables are crisp-tender, stirring halfway through cooking time. Sprinkle with remaining ⅔ *cup* onions. Microwave 1 minute or until onions are golden.

Makes 4 to 6 servings

Prep Time: 5 minutes
Cook Time: 10 minutes

*Or, bake in preheated 375°F oven 30 to 35 minutes.

Holiday Vegetable Bake

The Other Burger

■■■

1 pound ground pork, about 80% lean
1 teaspoon ground black pepper
¼ teaspoon salt

Gently mix together ground pork and seasonings. Shape into 4 burgers, each about ¾ inch thick. Place over moderately hot coals in kettle-style grill. Cover and grill for 5 minutes; turn and finish grilling 4 to 5 minutes more or until no longer pink in center. Serve immediately on sandwich buns, if desired.

Makes 4 servings

Eastern Burger: To Other Burger basic mix, add 2 tablespoons dry sherry, 1 tablespoon grated ginger root and 2 teaspoons soy sauce.

South-of-the-Border Burger: To Other Burger basic mix, add ¼ teaspoon *each* ground cumin, oregano, seasoned salt and crushed red chilies.

Prep Time: 10 minutes
Cook Time: 10 minutes

Favorite recipe from **National Pork Producers Council**

Raspberry-Glazed Turkey

■■■

½ cup SMUCKER'S® Seedless Red Raspberry Jam
6 tablespoons raspberry vinegar
¼ cup Dijon mustard
4 small turkey breast tenderloins

In large saucepan, stir together jam, vinegar and mustard. Bring to a boil over high heat; cook and stir 3 minutes. Reserve about ½ cup glaze; coat turkey with some of remaining glaze.

Set turkey on rack in broiler pan. Broil about 4 inches from heat 15 to 20 minutes or until no longer pink in center, turning and basting once with remaining glaze.

Slice turkey crosswise. Serve with reserved glaze.

Makes 4 to 6 servings

Cook's Nook

Because it is low in fat, turkey is masquerading as everything from bologna to hot dogs to ham. Ground turkey and fresh turkey parts are finding their way to the dinner table with increasing frequency.

Smoky Kale Chiffonade

¾ pound fresh young kale or mustard greens
3 slices bacon
2 tablespoons crumbled blue cheese
Kumquat slices for garnish

1. Rinse kale well in large bowl of warm water; place in colander. Drain.

2. Discard any discolored leaves. To trim away tough stem ends, make "V-shaped" cut at stem end; discard tough stems.

3. To prepare a chiffonade, roll up 1 leaf jelly-roll fashion. Slice crosswise into ½-inch-thick slices; separate into strips. Repeat with remaining leaves. Set aside.

4. Cook bacon in medium skillet over medium heat until crisp. Remove bacon to paper towel. Add reserved kale to drippings in skillet. Cook and stir over medium-high heat 2 to 3 minutes or until wilted and tender (older leaves may take slightly longer).*

5. Crumble bacon. Toss bacon and blue cheese with kale. Transfer to warm serving dish. Garnish, if desired. Serve immediately.

Makes 4 side-dish servings

*If using mustard greens, stir-fry 4 to 6 minutes or until wilted and tender.

Smoky Kale Chiffonade

California-Style Wild Rice Pilaf

▐▐▐

1 cup uncooked brown and wild rice mix or other wild rice blend
1 package (9 ounces) DOLE® California Style Vegetables*
1 teaspoon dried basil leaves, crushed

*Cut cauliflower into smaller pieces, if desired.

• Cook rice as package directs, stirring in vegetables, seasoning packet and basil during last 3 minutes of cooking time.

• Drain excess liquid from vegetable-rice mixture. Spoon into serving dish. Garnish with fresh herbs, if desired.

Makes 6 servings

Prep Time: 5 minutes
Cook Time: 25 minutes

Serve It With Style!

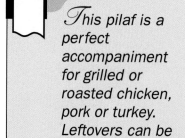

This pilaf is a perfect accompaniment for grilled or roasted chicken, pork or turkey. Leftovers can be easily reheated in the microwave.

Pretzels with a Chicken Twist

▐▐▐

2 packages BUTTERBALL® Chicken Breast Tenders, halved lengthwise
½ cup prepared honey mustard
2 cups crushed pretzels

Preheat oven to 400°F. Pour honey mustard into shallow bowl. Add chicken tenders and turn to coat. Discard any remaining honey mustard. Roll coated chicken in crushed pretzels. Place on baking sheet sprayed with nonstick cooking spray. Bake 5 to 8 minutes or until chicken is no longer pink in center. Serve with extra honey mustard for dipping.

Makes 32 appetizers

Preparation Time: 15 minutes

Sunshine Chicken Drumsticks

▌▌▌

½ cup A.1.® Steak Sauce
¼ cup ketchup
¼ cup apricot preserves
12 chicken drumsticks (about 2½ pounds)

In small bowl, using wire whisk, blend steak sauce, ketchup and preserves until smooth. Brush chicken with sauce.

Grill chicken over medium heat for 20 minutes or until no longer pink near bone, turning and brushing with remaining sauce. *(Do not baste during last 5 minutes of grilling.)* Serve hot.

Makes 12 appetizers

Santa Fe Rice

▌▌▌

2½ cups hot cooked MINUTE® Original Rice
1 cup canned black *or* red beans
1 cup TACO BELL HOME ORIGINALS® Thick 'N Chunky Salsa

MIX all ingredients. Serve immediately.

Makes 4 servings

Prep Time: 10 minutes

Veggie Tuna Pasta

▌▌▌

1 package (16 ounces) medium pasta shells
1 bag (16 ounces) BIRDS EYE® frozen Farm Fresh Mixtures Broccoli, Corn & Red Peppers
1 can (10 ounces) chunky light tuna, packed in water
1 can (10¾ ounces) reduced-fat cream of mushroom soup

• In large saucepan, cook pasta according to package directions. Add vegetables during last 10 minutes; drain and return to saucepan.

• Stir in tuna and soup. Add salt and pepper to taste. Cook over medium heat until heated through. *Makes 4 servings*

Variation: Stir in 1 can (4 to 6 ounces) chopped ripe olives with tuna.

Serving Suggestion: For a creamier dish, add a few tablespoons water; blend well.

Prep Time: 2 minutes
Cook Time: 12 to 15 minutes

Swiss Rosti Potatoes

███

4 large Russet potatoes
    (about 6 ounces each)*
4 tablespoons butter or
    margarine
Salt and pepper

*Prepare potatoes several hours or up to
1 day in advance.*

1. Preheat oven to 400°F. To prepare potatoes, pierce each potato in several places with fork. Bake 1 hour or until fork-tender. Cool completely, then refrigerate.

2. When potatoes are cold, peel with paring knife. Grate potatoes by hand with large section of metal grater or use food processor with large grater disk.

3. Heat butter in 10-inch skillet over medium-high heat until melted and bubbly. Press grated potatoes evenly into skillet. (Do not stir or turn potatoes.) Season with salt and pepper to taste. Cook 10 to 12 minutes until golden brown.

4. Turn off heat; invert serving plate over skillet. Turn potatoes out onto plate. Garnish, if desired. Serve immediately.

Makes 4 side-dish servings

Grilled Sausage with Apricot-Mustard Glaze

███

½ cup SMUCKER'S® Apricot
    Preserves
½ cup Dijon mustard
1 pound smoked pork
    sausage
4 French sandwich rolls

Combine preserves and mustard; blend well. Set aside.

Cut pork sausage into 2-inch pieces and place on baking sheet. Grill or broil 4 minutes; turn and cook another 4 minutes.

Remove baking sheet from heat and dip each piece in apricot-mustard glaze. Return to broiler or grill and cook 2 more minutes or until lightly browned. Divide among sandwich rolls; serve with additional apricot-mustard glaze on the side.

Makes 4 servings

SNAPPY

Skillet Suppers

Chicken Étouffé with Pasta

▮▮▮

- ¼ cup vegetable oil
- ⅓ cup all-purpose flour
- ½ cup finely chopped onion
- 4 boneless skinless chicken breast halves (about 1¼ pounds), cut into ¼-inch-thick strips
- 1 cup chicken broth
- 1 medium tomato, chopped
- ¾ cup sliced celery
- 1 medium green bell pepper, chopped
- 2 teaspoons Creole or Cajun seasoning blend
  Hot cooked pasta

1. Heat oil in large skillet over medium heat until hot. Add flour; cook and stir 10 minutes or until dark brown. Add onion. Cook and stir 2 minutes.

2. Stir in chicken, broth, tomato, celery, bell pepper and seasoning blend. Cook 8 minutes or until chicken is no longer pink in center. Serve over pasta.

Makes 6 servings

Prep and Cook Time: 25 minutes

Szechuan Vegetable Stir-Fry

▐▐▐

8 ounces firm tofu, drained
    and cut into cubes
1 cup canned vegetable
    broth, divided
½ cup orange juice
⅓ cup soy sauce
1 to 2 teaspoons hot chili oil
½ teaspoon fennel seeds
½ teaspoon ground black
    pepper
2 tablespoons cornstarch
3 tablespoons vegetable oil
1 cup sliced green onions and
    tops
3 medium carrots, peeled and
    diagonally sliced
3 cloves garlic, minced
2 teaspoons minced fresh
    ginger
¼ pound button mushrooms,
    sliced
1 medium red bell pepper,
    seeded and cut into
    1-inch squares
¼ pound fresh snow peas, cut
    diagonally in half
8 ounces broccoli florets,
    steamed
½ cup peanuts
4 to 6 cups hot cooked rice

1. Place tofu in 8-inch round or square glass baking dish. Combine ½ cup broth, orange juice, soy sauce, chili oil, fennel seeds and black pepper in 2-cup measure; pour over tofu. Let stand 15 to 60 minutes. Drain, reserving marinade.

2. Combine cornstarch and remaining ½ cup broth in medium bowl. Add reserved marinade; set aside.

3. Heat vegetable oil in wok or large skillet over high heat until hot. Add onions, carrots, garlic and ginger; stir-fry 3 minutes. Add tofu, mushrooms, bell pepper and snow peas; stir-fry 2 to 3 minutes or until vegetables are crisp-tender. Add broccoli; stir-fry 1 minute or until heated through.

4. Stir cornstarch mixture. Add to wok; cook 1 to 2 minutes or until bubbly. Stir in peanuts. Serve over rice.

Makes 4 to 6 servings

Szechuan Vegetable Stir-Fry

Walnut Chicken

▌▌▌

- **3 tablespoons soy sauce**
- **2 tablespoons minced fresh ginger**
- **1 tablespoon cornstarch**
- **1 tablespoon rice wine**
- **2 cloves garlic, minced**
- **¼ to ½ teaspoon red pepper flakes**
- **1 pound boneless skinless chicken thighs, diced**
- **3 tablespoons vegetable oil**
- **½ cup walnut halves or pieces**
- **1 cup frozen cut green beans, thawed**
- **½ cup sliced water chestnuts**
- **2 green onions with tops, cut into 1-inch pieces**
- **¼ cup water**
  Hot cooked rice

Combine soy sauce, ginger, cornstarch, wine, garlic and red pepper in large bowl; stir until smooth. Add chicken; toss. Marinate 10 minutes.

Heat wok or large skillet over high heat about 1 minute or until hot. Drizzle oil into wok and heat 30 seconds. Add walnuts; stir-fry about 1 minute or until lightly browned. Remove to small bowl. Add chicken mixture to wok; stir-fry about 5 to 7 minutes or until chicken is no longer pink in center. Add beans, water chestnuts, onions and water; stir-fry until heated through. Serve over rice. Sprinkle with walnuts.   *Makes 4 servings*

Walnut Chicken

Meatball Stroganoff with Rice

▌▌▌

MEATBALLS
 1 egg, lightly beaten
1½ pounds ground beef round
 ⅓ cup plain dry bread crumbs
 1 tablespoon Worcestershire
    sauce
 1 teaspoon salt
 ¼ teaspoon pepper
 2 tablespoons CRISCO®
    Vegetable Oil

SAUCE
 1 tablespoon CRISCO®
    Vegetable Oil
 ½ pound mushrooms, sliced
 2 tablespoons all-purpose
    flour
 1 teaspoon ketchup
 1 can (10½ ounces)
    condensed, double
    strength beef broth
    (bouillon), undiluted*
 ½ (1-ounce) envelope dry
    onion soup mix (about
    2 tablespoons)
 1 cup sour cream

 4 cups hot cooked rice

* 1¼ cups reconstituted beef broth made
with double amount of very low sodium
beef broth granules may be substituted
for beef broth (bouillon).

1. For meatballs, combine egg, meat, bread crumbs, Worcestershire sauce, salt and pepper in large bowl. Mix until well blended. Shape into eighteen 2-inch meatballs.

2. Heat 2 tablespoons Crisco® Oil in large skillet on medium heat. Add meatballs. Brown on all sides. Reduce heat to low. Cook 10 minutes. Remove meatballs from skillet.

3. For sauce, add 1 tablespoon Crisco® Oil to skillet. Add mushrooms. Cook and stir 4 minutes. Remove skillet from heat.

4. Stir in flour and ketchup until blended. Stir in broth gradually. Add soup mix. Return to heat. Bring to a boil on medium heat. Reduce heat to low. Simmer 2 minutes. Return meatballs to skillet. Heat thoroughly, stirring occasionally.

5. Stir in sour cream. Heat but do not bring to a boil. Serve over hot rice. Garnish, if desired.   *Makes 6 servings*

White Chili

▌▌▌

1 pound ground turkey
2 cloves garlic, finely
    chopped
2 cans (15 ounces each)
    white kidney beans,
    undrained
2 cans (4 ounces each)
    chopped green chilies,
    undrained
1⅓ cups FRENCH'S® French
    Fried Onions, divided
1 cup frozen whole kernel
    corn
¼ cup chopped fresh cilantro
3 tablespoons lime juice
1 tablespoon ground cumin
¼ teaspoon ground white
    pepper
1 large tomato, chopped
¼ cup low-fat sour cream

Heat large nonstick skillet or
Dutch oven over medium heat.
Add turkey and garlic; cook and
stir about 5 minutes or until
turkey is no longer pink.

Stir in beans, green chilies, ⅔
cup French Fried Onions, corn,
cilantro, lime juice, cumin and
white pepper. Bring to a boil
over high heat. Reduce heat to
low; simmer 5 minutes, stirring
often.

Stir in tomato and sour cream;
cook until hot and bubbly,
stirring often. Sprinkle with
remaining ⅔ *cup* onions.
Makes 4 to 6 servings

Prep Time: 15 minutes
Cook Time: 20 minutes

Mexican Skillet Rice

▌▌▌

¾ pound lean ground pork or
    lean ground beef
1 medium onion, chopped
1½ tablespoons chili powder
1 teaspoon ground cumin
½ teaspoon salt
3 cups cooked brown rice
1 can (16 ounces) pinto
    beans, drained
2 cans (4 ounces each) diced
    green chilies
1 medium tomato, seeded
    and chopped (optional)

Cook meat in large skillet over
medium-high heat until brown,
stirring to crumble; drain.
Return meat to skillet. Add
onion, chili powder, cumin and
salt; cook until onion is soft but
not brown. Stir in rice, beans
and chilies; thoroughly heat.
Top with tomato.
Makes 6 servings

Mexican Skillet Rice

Bratwurst Skillet

■ ■ ■

1 pound bratwurst links, cut into ½-inch slices
1½ cups green bell pepper strips
1½ cups red bell pepper strips
1½ cups sliced onions
1 teaspoon paprika
1 teaspoon caraway seeds

1. Heat large skillet over medium heat until hot. Add bratwurst; cover and cook about 5 minutes or until browned and no longer pink in center. Transfer bratwurst to plate. Cover and keep warm.

2. Drain all but 1 tablespoon drippings from skillet. Add bell peppers, onions, paprika and caraway seeds. Cook and stir about 5 minutes or until vegetables are tender.

3. Combine bratwurst and vegetables. Serve immediately.
Makes 4 servings

Cutting Corners: To make this even speedier, purchase a packaged stir-fry pepper and onion mix and use in place of the bell peppers and onions.

Prep and Cook Time:
18 minutes

Frittata Primavera

■ ■ ■

1 medium onion, chopped
1 medium red or green bell pepper, cut into strips
1 medium potato, peeled and grated (about 1 cup)
1 cup coarsely chopped broccoli
1 teaspoon dried oregano leaves, crushed
⅛ teaspoon ground black pepper
1 tablespoon FLEISCHMANN'S® Original Spread (70% Corn Oil)
1 (8-ounce) container EGG BEATERS® Healthy Real Egg Substitute

In 10-inch nonstick skillet or omelet pan, cook and stir onion, bell pepper, potato, broccoli, oregano and black pepper in spread until vegetables are tender-crisp.

In small bowl, with electric mixer at high speed, beat Egg Beaters® for 2 minutes until light and fluffy; pour over vegetables. Cover and cook over medium heat for 5 to 7 minutes until eggs are set. Serve from pan or carefully invert onto warm serving plate. Serve immediately.
Makes 4 servings

Chicken Paprikash

▌▌▌

3 tablespoons butter
3½ cups thinly sliced onions
2 cups red bell pepper strips
4 large cloves garlic, minced
2½ tablespoons all-purpose flour
4 teaspoons paprika
2 cups chicken broth
2 tablespoons tomato paste
1½ pounds boneless skinless chicken breasts, trimmed and cut into 1-inch strips
Salt and pepper to taste
1 cup sour cream
1 pound cooked extra-wide egg noodles
1 tablespoon minced parsley

Melt butter in large skillet over medium heat. Add onions, bell peppers and garlic; stir well. Cover and cook 15 minutes, stirring occasionally. Do not let vegetables brown; reduce heat if necessary. Stir in flour and paprika. Cook and stir 1 to 2 minutes, until completely blended. Add chicken broth and tomato paste; stir. Increase heat to medium. Cook and stir until sauce comes to a boil. Add chicken. Stir until mixture returns to a boil. Reduce heat to low. Cover and cook 15 to 20 minutes or until chicken is no longer pink in center, stirring occasionally. Season with salt and pepper to taste.

Place sour cream in small bowl. Slowly pour ¼ cup thickened sauce into sour cream, stirring constantly until blended. Repeat with additional ¼ cup. Slowly pour sour cream mixture back into skillet, stirring constantly to prevent sour cream from separating. Serve immediately over hot noodles. Sprinkle with parsley.

Makes 6 servings

Beef with Cabbage and Carrots

▌▌▌

¾ pound extra-lean (90% lean) ground beef
4 cups shredded cabbage
1½ cups shredded carrot (1 large carrot)
½ teaspoon caraway seeds
2 tablespoons seasoned rice vinegar
Salt and freshly ground pepper

Brown ground beef in large skillet. Drain. Reduce heat to low. Stir in cabbage, carrot and caraway seeds; cover. Cook 10 minutes or until vegetables are tender, stirring occasionally. Stir in vinegar. (Add 1 tablespoon water for extra moistness, if desired.) Season with salt and pepper to taste.

Makes 4 servings

Teriyaki Beef

███

¾ pound sirloin tip steak, cut
    into thin strips
½ cup teriyaki sauce
¼ cup water
1 tablespoon cornstarch
1 teaspoon sugar
1 bag (16 ounces) BIRDS
    EYE® frozen Farm Fresh
    Mixtures Broccoli,
    Carrots and Water
    Chestnuts

• Spray large skillet with
nonstick cooking spray; cook
beef strips over medium-high
heat 7 to 8 minutes, stirring
occasionally.

• Combine teriyaki sauce,
water, cornstarch and sugar;
mix well.

• Add teriyaki sauce mixture
and vegetables to beef. Bring to
boil; quickly reduce heat to
medium.

• Cook 7 to 10 minutes or until
broccoli is heated through,
stirring occasionally.
Makes 4 to 6 servings

Prep Time: 5 to 10 minutes
Cook Time: 20 minutes

Cajun Pork Skillet Dinner

███

1 tablespoon vegetable oil
4 rib-cut pork chops* (about
    1 pound), cut ¾ inch
    thick
1 jar (16 ounces) chunky
    medium salsa
1⅓ cups FRENCH'S® French
    Fried Onions, divided
½ teaspoon dried thyme
    leaves
    Cooked white rice
    (optional)

Or, substitute 1 pound boneless skinless chicken breasts for pork chops.

Heat oil in large nonstick skillet.
Add pork chops; cook about 5
minutes or until browned on
both sides.

Stir in salsa, *⅔ cup* French Fried
Onions and thyme. Bring to a
boil over high heat. Reduce
heat to medium-low. Cover;
cook 10 minutes or until pork
is no longer pink near bone,
stirring occasionally. Sprinkle
remaining *⅔ cup* onions over
pork. Serve with rice, if desired.
Makes 4 servings

Tip: For a Mediterranean flair,
substitute ½ teaspoon oregano
for ½ teaspoon thyme.

Prep Time: 5 minutes
Cook Time: 15 minutes

Manhattan Turkey à la King

▌▌▌

8 ounces wide egg noodles
1 pound boneless turkey or
    chicken, cut into strips
1 tablespoon vegetable oil
1 can (14½ ounces) DEL
    MONTE® Pasta Style
    Chunky Tomatoes
1 can (10¾ ounces)
    condensed cream of
    celery soup
1 medium onion, chopped
2 stalks celery, sliced
1 cup sliced mushrooms

1. Cook noodles according to package directions; drain. In large skillet, brown turkey in oil over medium-high heat. Season with salt and pepper, if desired.

2. Add remaining ingredients, except noodles. Cover and cook over medium heat 5 minutes.

3. Remove cover; cook 5 minutes or until thickened, stirring occasionally. Serve over hot noodles. Garnish with chopped parsley, if desired.

Makes 6 servings

Hint: Cook pasta ahead; rinse and drain. Cover and refrigerate. Just before serving, heat in microwave or dip in boiling water.

Prep Time: 7 minutes
Cook Time: 20 minutes

Chicken Carbonara

▌▌▌

1 pound chicken tenders
1 jar (12 ounces) Alfredo
    sauce
1 cup milk
1⅓ cups FRENCH'S® French
    Fried Onions, divided
½ of a 10-ounce package
    frozen peas, thawed and
    drained
2 tablespoons real bacon
    bits*
Hot cooked pasta

*Or, substitute 2 strips crumbled, cooked bacon for real bacon bits.

Spray large nonstick skillet with nonstick cooking spray; heat over high heat. Add chicken; cook and stir about 5 minutes or until browned.

Stir in Alfredo sauce and milk. Add ⅔ cup French Fried Onions, peas and bacon bits. Bring to a boil. Reduce heat to low. Cook 5 minutes, stirring occasionally. Serve over pasta. Sprinkle with remaining ⅔ cup onions.

Makes 4 to 6 servings

Prep Time: 10 minutes
Cook Time: 10 minutes

Eggplant and Feta Skillet

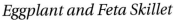

¼ cup olive oil
1 medium eggplant, cut into 1-inch pieces
1 medium zucchini, cut into ½-inch slices
1 package (16 ounces) frozen bell peppers and onions blend, thawed and drained
2 teaspoons bottled minced garlic
2 cans (14½ ounces each) Italian-style diced tomatoes, drained
1 can (2¼ ounces) sliced black olives, drained
1½ cups prepared croutons
¾ cup feta cheese with basil and tomato, crumbled

1. Heat oil in large skillet over high heat until hot.

2. Add eggplant, zucchini, stir-fry blend and garlic; cook and stir 6 minutes. Add tomatoes; simmer 3 minutes. Stir in olives.

3. Sprinkle croutons and feta cheese over top.

Makes 6 servings

Prep and Cook Time:
20 minutes

Eggplant and Feta Skillet

Spicy Mexican Frittata

▌▌▌

1 fresh jalapeño pepper
1 clove garlic
1 medium tomato, peeled, halved, seeded and quartered
½ teaspoon ground coriander
½ teaspoon chili powder
½ cup chopped onion
1 cup frozen corn
6 egg whites
2 eggs
¼ cup skim milk
¼ teaspoon salt
¼ teaspoon black pepper
¼ cup (1 ounce) shredded part-skim farmer or mozzarella cheese

Add jalapeño pepper and garlic to food processor or blender. Process until finely chopped. Add tomato, coriander and chili powder. Cover; process until tomato is almost smooth.

Spray large skillet with nonstick cooking spray; heat skillet over medium heat. Cook and stir onion in hot skillet until tender. Stir in tomato mixture and corn. Cook 3 to 4 minutes or until liquid is almost evaporated, stirring occasionally.

Combine egg whites, eggs, milk, salt and black pepper in medium bowl. Add egg mixture all at once to skillet. Cook, without stirring, 2 minutes or until eggs begin to set. Run large spoon around edge of skillet, lifting eggs for even cooking. Remove skillet from heat when eggs are almost set but surface is still moist.

Sprinkle with cheese. Cover; let stand 3 to 4 minutes or until surface is set and cheese melts. Cut into wedges.

Makes 4 servings

Ham Scramble

▌▌▌

2 tablespoons vegetable oil or butter
1 pound HILLSHIRE FARM® Ham, cut into bite-size pieces
2 onions, thinly sliced
2 apples, cored and sliced

Heat oil in large skillet over medium-high heat. Sauté Ham, onions and apples until onions and apples are tender, stirring constantly.

Makes 4 to 6 servings

Spicy Mexican Frittata

Hearty Hot Dish

▌▌▌

⅓ cup honey
¼ cup spicy brown mustard
¼ cup vegetable oil
1 tablespoon soy sauce
2 cloves garlic, minced
1 teaspoon ground ginger
1 pound HILLSHIRE FARM®
      Beef Smoked Sausage,*
      sliced
2 onions, cut into quarters
1 cup chopped carrots
1 cup chopped celery
1 cup sliced mushrooms

*Or use any variety Hillshire Farm®
Smoked Sausage.*

Combine honey, mustard, oil,
soy sauce, garlic and ginger in
large bowl; blend thoroughly.
Add Smoked Sausage, onions,
carrots, celery and mushrooms.
Saute sausage mixture in large
skillet over medium-high heat
until sausage is lightly
browned.

Makes 4 to 6 servings

Tuna and Rice Skillet Dinner

▌▌▌

1 package (6½ ounces)
      chicken flavored rice mix
½ cup chopped onion
      Water
1½ cups frozen peas and
      carrots, thawed
1 can (10¾ ounces) cream of
      mushroom soup
⅛ teaspoon ground black
      pepper
1 can (12 ounces) STARKIST®
      Solid White or Chunk
      Light Tuna, drained and
      chunked
⅓ cup toasted slivered
      almonds (optional)

In medium saucepan, combine
rice mix and onion; add water.
Prepare rice according to
package directions. Stir in
vegetables, soup and pepper;
blend well. Simmer, covered,
5 to 7 minutes, stirring
occasionally. Stir in tuna; serve
with almonds, if desired.

Makes 4 to 6 servings

Prep Time: 30 minutes

Cook's Notes

When buying new baking
dishes and pans, choose
pieces you can use for
more than one job. For
instance, skillets should
be able to go into
the oven.

Hearty Hot Dish

PIZZA

IN A PINCH

Chicken-Pesto Pizza

8 ounces chicken tenders
1 medium onion, thinly sliced
⅓ cup prepared pesto
3 medium plum tomatoes, thinly sliced
1 (14-inch) prepared pizza crust
1 cup (4 ounces) shredded mozzarella cheese

1. Preheat oven to 450°F. Cut chicken tenders into bite-size pieces. Coat medium nonstick skillet with nonstick cooking spray; cook and stir chicken over medium heat 2 minutes. Add onion and pesto; cook and stir about 3 minutes or until chicken is cooked through.

2. Arrange tomato slices and chicken mixture on pizza crust to within 1 inch of edge. Sprinkle cheese over topping. Bake 8 minutes or until pizza is hot and cheese is melted and bubbly. *Makes 6 servings*

Prep and Cook Time:
22 minutes

Niçoise Pizza

▮▮▮

4 ounces goat cheese
½ cup ricotta cheese
½ cup minced fresh basil
1 teaspoon black pepper
1 purchased bread or pizza
     crust (16-ounce size)
2 tablespoons olive oil,
     divided
1 large red onion, sliced
¼ pound fresh young green
     beans, diagonally sliced
1 yellow or red bell pepper,
     cut into thin strips
3 tablespoons sliced black
     olives
½ cup freshly grated
     Parmesan cheese

1. Combine goat cheese, ricotta cheese, basil and black pepper until blended. Spread on bread crust to within ½ inch of edge. Set aside.

2. Preheat oven to 450°F. Heat 1 tablespoon oil in large skillet over medium heat until hot.

3. Add onion to skillet. Cook and stir 8 to 10 minutes or until onion is very tender and brown. Arrange on top of cheese mixture.

4. Heat remaining 1 tablespoon olive oil in same skillet over medium heat until hot. Add beans; cook and stir 1 minute. Add bell pepper; cook and stir

1 minute or until crisp-tender. Arrange on top of onion.

5. Top with olives; sprinkle with Parmesan cheese. Bake 8 to 10 minutes or until bread crust is heated through. Garnish, if desired.   *Makes 4 servings*

Pizza Romano

▮▮▮

1 (10-inch) prepared pizza
     crust *or* 4 rounds pita
     bread
1 cup (4 ounces) shredded
     mozzarella cheese
4 slices HILLSHIRE FARM®
     Ham, cut into ½-inch
     strips
1 jar (8 ounces) marinated
     sun-dried tomatoes,
     drained (optional)
1 jar (6 ounces) oil-packed
     artichokes, drained and
     cut into eighths
1 jar (4 ounces) roasted red
     peppers, drained and cut
     into strips

Preheat oven to 425°F.

Place pizza crust on cookie sheet; top with remaining ingredients. Bake on lower rack of oven 15 to 20 minutes or until crust begins to brown lightly and cheese is melted.
      Makes 4 servings

BBQ Beef Pizza

###

½ pound lean ground beef
1 medium green bell pepper
⅔ cup prepared barbecue
  sauce
1 (14-inch) prepared pizza
  crust
3 to 4 onion slices, rings
  separated
½ (2¼-ounce) can sliced
  black olives, drained
1 cup (4 ounces) shredded
  cheese (Colby and
  Monterey Jack mix)

1. Preheat oven to 400°F. Place meat in large skillet; cook over high heat 6 to 8 minutes or until meat is no longer pink, breaking meat apart with wooden spoon. Pour off drippings; remove from heat.

2. While meat is cooking, seed bell pepper and slice into ¼-inch-thick rings. Add barbecue sauce to cooked meat in skillet. Place pizza crust on baking pan. Spread meat mixture over pizza crust to within ½ inch of edge. Arrange onion slices and pepper rings over meat. Sprinkle with olives and cheese. Bake 8 minutes or until cheese is melted. Cut into 8 wedges.

Makes 3 to 4 servings

Prep and Cook Time:
20 minutes

South-of-the-Border Pizza

###

1 prepared pizza shell or crust
  (about 12 inches)
1 cup cooked low-sodium
  kidney beans, rinsed and
  drained
1 cup frozen whole kernel
  corn, thawed
1 tomato, chopped
¼ cup finely chopped fresh
  cilantro
1 jalapeño pepper, finely
  chopped
¼ cup (4 ounces) shredded
  reduced-fat Monterey
  Jack cheese

1. Preheat oven to 450°F. Place pizza shell on *ungreased* pizza pan or baking sheet.

2. Arrange beans, corn, tomato, cilantro and jalapeño over pizza shell. Sprinkle evenly with cheese.

3. Bake pizza 8 to 10 minutes or until cheese is melted and lightly browned. Garnish with green bell pepper, if desired.

Makes 4 servings

California Thin Crust Pizza with Smoked Turkey

▌▌▌

1 BUTTERBALL® Fully Cooked Smoked Young Turkey, thawed, sliced thin
½ cup mayonnaise
3 tablespoons grated Parmesan cheese
1 tube (10 ounces) prepared pizza dough
1 teaspoon dried oregano, divided
¼ cup sun-dried tomato bits packed in oil
1 can (14 ounces) artichoke hearts, drained and chopped
1 cup crumbled feta cheese

Combine mayonnaise and Parmesan cheese in small bowl; set aside. Spray 15×10-inch jelly-roll pan with nonstick cooking spray. Press dough into pan. Sprinkle dough with ½ teaspoon oregano. Bake in preheated 425°F oven 8 to 10 minutes or until crust begins to brown. Remove from oven; spread with mayonnaise mixture. Sprinkle turkey, tomato, artichokes and cheese on top of crust. Top with remaining ½ teaspoon oregano. Bake 10 to 12 minutes longer until toppings are heated through.

Makes 24 appetizers

Grilled Vegetables Pizza

▌▌▌

1 teaspoon salt
2 cups (¼-inch) zucchini slices
10 (¼-inch) eggplant slices
2 tablespoons olive oil
1 (12-inch) BOBOLI® Brand Italian Bread Shell
1 cup KRAFT® Shredded Low-Moisture Part-Skim Mozzarella Cheese, divided
¼ cup (¼-inch) roasted red pepper slices
1 tablespoon coarsely chopped fresh basil leaves

Preheat grill. Lightly salt zucchini and eggplant. Brush with oil. Grill on both sides until tender. Sprinkle Boboli® Italian bread shell with ½ cup cheese. Top with grilled vegetables, roasted red peppers, basil and remaining ½ cup cheese. Place bread shell on grill 5 inches from coals. Cover and grill for 3 to 4 minutes or until cheese is melted.

Makes 4 to 6 servings

California Thin Crust Pizza with Smoked Turkey

Pesto Dijon Pizza

III

½ cup chopped parsley*
⅓ cup GREY POUPON® Dijon Mustard
¼ cup PLANTERS® Walnuts, chopped*
1 tablespoon olive oil*
2 tablespoons grated Parmesan cheese,* divided
1½ teaspoons dried basil leaves,* divided
2 (8-ounce) packages small prepared pizza crusts
4 ounces thinly sliced deli baked ham
3 plum tomatoes, sliced
1 cup shredded mozzarella cheese (4 ounces)

1 (7-ounce) container prepared pesto sauce may be substituted for parsley, walnuts, olive oil, 1 tablespoon Parmesan cheese and 1 teaspoon basil. Stir mustard into prepared pesto sauce.

In small bowl, combine parsley, mustard, walnuts, oil, 1 tablespoon Parmesan cheese and 1 teaspoon basil. Divide mixture and spread evenly onto each pizza crust. Top each crust with 2 ounces ham, tomato slices and mozzarella cheese. Sprinkle with remaining Parmesan cheese and basil. Place on baking sheet. Bake at 450°F for 8 to 10 minutes or until cheese melts. Cut into wedges; serve warm.

Makes 4 servings

Quattro Formaggio Pizza

III

1 (12-inch) Italian bread shell
½ cup prepared pizza or marinara sauce
4 ounces shaved or thinly sliced provolone cheese
1 cup (4 ounces) shredded smoked or regular mozzarella cheese
2 ounces asiago or brick cheese, thinly sliced
¼ cup freshly grated Parmesan or Romano cheese

1. Heat oven to 450°F.

2. Place bread shell on baking sheet. Spread pizza sauce evenly over bread shell.

3. Top sauce with provolone, mozzarella, asiago and Parmesan cheese.

4. Bake 14 minutes or until bread shell is golden brown and cheese is melted.

5. Cut into wedges; serve immediately.

Makes 4 servings

Serving Suggestion: Serve with a tossed green salad.

Prep and Cook Time: 26 minutes

Pesto Dijon Pizza

Classic Potato, Onion & Ham Pizza

▌▌▌

3 tablespoons butter or olive oil, divided
3 cups new potatoes, cut into ¼-inch slices
2 sweet onions, cut into ¼-inch slices
1 tablespoon coarsely chopped garlic
½ teaspoon salt
½ teaspoon black pepper
2 cups (8 ounces) shredded Wisconsin Mozzarella cheese
1 (16-ounce) Italian-style bread shell pizza crust
8 thin slices (4 ounces) deli ham
8 slices (4 ounces) Wisconsin Provolone cheese
⅓ cup grated Wisconsin Parmesan cheese
¼ cup chopped Italian parsley

Melt 2 tablespoons butter in large skillet over medium heat; add potatoes, onions, garlic, salt and pepper. Cook 12 to 15 minutes, turning occasionally. Add remaining 1 tablespoon butter. Cook 5 to 7 minutes or until potatoes are golden brown. Cool slightly.

Preheat oven to 400°F. Sprinkle mozzarella cheese over crust; top with ham slices. Arrange potato mixture over ham; top with provolone cheese. Sprinkle with Parmesan cheese and parsley. Place crust directly on oven rack; bake 15 to 20 minutes or until cheese is melted. *Makes 4 servings*

Favorite recipe from Wisconsin Milk Marketing Board

Herbed Mushroom Pizza

▌▌▌

2 tablespoons olive oil
8 ounces sliced button or wild mushrooms, such as portobello or shiitake
1½ teaspoons bottled minced garlic
½ teaspoon dried basil leaves
½ teaspoon dried thyme leaves
¼ teaspoon salt
¼ teaspoon black pepper
⅓ cup pizza or marinara sauce
1 (12-inch)bread-style pizza crust
1½ cups (6 ounces) shredded mozzarella cheese

1. Preheat oven to 450°F. Heat oil in large skillet over medium-high heat until hot. Add mushrooms and garlic; cook 4 minutes, stirring occasionally. Stir in basil, thyme, salt and pepper.

2. Spread pizza sauce evenly over crust. Top with mushroom mixture; sprinkle with cheese. Bake directly on oven rack 8 minutes or until crust is golden brown and cheese is melted. Slide cookie sheet under pizza to remove from oven.

Makes 4 servings

Prep and Cook Time:
15 minutes

Marinated Chicken and Pesto Pizza

█ █ █

8 ounces chicken tenders
¼ cup prepared fat-free Italian salad dressing
Nonstick cooking spray
½ cup sun-dried tomatoes
1 cup chopped Roma tomatoes
1 tablespoon prepared pesto
1 teaspoon salt-free Italian herb blend
¼ teaspoon crushed red pepper
1 (12-inch) prepared pizza crust
1 cup (4 ounces) shredded part-skim mozzarella cheese

1. Cut chicken tenders into 2×½-inch strips. Place in resealable plastic food storage bag. Pour Italian dressing over chicken, turning to coat. Seal bag. Marinate at room temperature 15 minutes, turning several times. Remove chicken from marinade; discard marinade. Spray large nonstick skillet with cooking spray; heat over medium heat until hot. Add chicken; cook and stir 5 minutes or until no longer pink in center.

2. Cover sun-dried tomatoes with boiling water in small bowl; let stand 10 minutes. Drain; cut tomatoes into ¼-inch strips.

3. Preheat oven to 450°F. Combine Roma tomatoes, pesto, herb blend and pepper in small bowl. Spread on pizza crust. Add chicken tenders and sun-dried tomatoes; sprinkle with cheese.

4. Bake 8 to 10 minutes or until cheese melts and pizza is heated through. Cut into slices.

Makes 6 servings

Pizza with Fontina, Artichoke Hearts and Red Onion

███

1 pound frozen white bread dough, thawed according to package directions
2 tablespoons olive oil, divided
2 tablespoons wheat bran
1 large clove garlic, minced
½ red onion, thinly sliced
1 package (9 ounces) frozen artichoke hearts, thawed and sliced lengthwise
Salt and black pepper
1 cup (4 ounces) shredded Wisconsin Fontina cheese

Preheat oven to 450°F. On lightly oiled baking sheet, press chilled dough into 12×9-inch rectangle; crimp edges to form rim. Brush with 1 tablespoon oil. Evenly sprinkle with bran; press lightly into dough. Sprinkle with garlic. Arrange onion in 1 layer over dough; top with artichoke hearts. Drizzle with remaining 1 tablespoon oil. Lightly season with salt and pepper. Evenly sprinkle with cheese. (Do not let dough rise.) Bake 15 minutes or until crust is golden brown.

Makes 4 servings

Favorite recipe from **Wisconsin Milk Marketing Board**

Barbecue Pizza

███

2 teaspoons olive oil
1 boneless skinless chicken breast (about 5 ounces), cut into ¾-inch cubes
3 ounces HILLSHIRE FARM® Pepperoni, sliced
⅓ cup barbecue sauce, divided
1 (12-inch) prepared pizza crust
1¼ cups shredded mozzarella cheese, divided
2 tablespoons thinly sliced green onion tops

Preheat oven to 450°F.

Heat oil in small skillet over medium-high heat. Sauté chicken until barely done, 3 to 5 minutes. Remove from heat and pour off juices. Add Pepperoni and 1 tablespoon barbecue sauce to chicken. Stir to mix and separate slices.

Spread remaining barbecue sauce over pizza crust. Sprinkle ¾ cup cheese over sauce. Sprinkle pepperoni mixture over cheese; sprinkle with green onion. Top with remaining ½ cup cheese. Place in oven directly on oven rack. Bake 8 to 10 minutes or until cheese is bubbly and pizza crust is crisp.

Makes 4 to 6 servings

Barbecue Pizza

Pita Pizzas

Nonstick cooking spray
½ pound boneless skinless chicken breasts, cubed
½ cup sliced red bell pepper
½ cup sliced mushrooms
½ cup thinly sliced red onion
2 cloves garlic, minced
1 teaspoon dried basil leaves
½ teaspoon dried oregano leaves
1 cup torn fresh spinach leaves
6 mini whole wheat pita breads
½ cup (2 ounces) shredded part-skim mozzarella cheese
1 tablespoon grated Parmesan cheese

1. Preheat oven to 375°F. Spray medium nonstick skillet with cooking spray; heat over medium heat until hot. Add chicken; cook and stir 6 minutes or until browned and no longer pink in center. Remove chicken from skillet.

2. Spray same nonstick skillet again with cooking spray; add bell pepper, mushrooms, onion, garlic, basil and oregano. Cook and stir over medium heat 5 to 7 minutes or until vegetables are crisp-tender. Return chicken to skillet.

Pita Pizzas

3. Place spinach on top of pita breads. Divide chicken and vegetable mixture evenly; spoon over spinach. Sprinkle evenly with mozzarella and Parmesan cheeses. Bake, uncovered, 7 to 10 minutes or until cheese is melted.

Makes 6 servings

Roasted Vegetable Pizza

▌▌▌

1 cup uncooked white rice
  Olive oil-flavored nonstick cooking spray
½ cup grated Parmesan cheese
2 egg whites, lightly beaten
1 pound eggplant, peeled and diced
1 large red or purple onion, thinly sliced
1 large red bell pepper, cut into 1-inch pieces
2 tablespoons Italian seasoning
1 can (6 ounces) no-salt-added tomato paste
2 tablespoons balsamic vinegar
¼ teaspoon garlic salt
1 cup (4 ounces) shredded part-skim mozzarella cheese
⅓ cup grated Parmesan cheese

1. Place 2 cups water in medium saucepan; bring to a boil over high heat. Stir in rice. Cover; reduce heat to low. Simmer 20 minutes or until liquid is absorbed. Cool completely.

2. Preheat oven to 450°F. Spray 12-inch nonstick pizza pan and 15×10-inch jelly-roll pan with cooking spray.

3. Stir ½ cup Parmesan cheese into rice; stir in egg whites until well blended. Spread into prepared pizza pan; set aside.

4. Place vegetables in large resealable plastic food storage bag. Generously spray with cooking spray; add Italian seasoning. Seal bag; toss to coat. Place vegetables on prepared jelly-roll pan. Bake 30 minutes or until vegetables are tender, stirring after 15 minutes.

5. *Reduce oven temperature to 400°F.* Combine tomato paste, vinegar and garlic salt in large bowl. Add vegetables; toss to coat. Spoon vegetables over rice.

6. Bake 10 minutes. Sprinkle with cheeses; bake 8 minutes or until cheeses are lightly browned. Garnish as desired.

Makes 12 appetizers

Thai Chicken Pizza

▌▌▌

2 boneless skinless chicken
   breast halves (½ pound)
2 teaspoons Thai seasoning
   Nonstick cooking spray
2 tablespoons pineapple juice
1 tablespoon peanut butter
1 tablespoon oyster sauce
1 teaspoon Thai chili paste*
2 (10-inch) flour tortillas
½ cup shredded carrot
½ cup sliced green onions
½ cup red bell pepper slices
¼ cup chopped cilantro
½ cup (2 ounces) shredded
   part-skim mozzarella
   cheese

Thai chili paste is available at some larger supermarkets and at Oriental markets.

1. Preheat oven to 400°F. Cut chicken breasts crosswise into thin slices, each about 1½×½ inch. Sprinkle with Thai seasoning. Let stand 5 minutes. Spray large nonstick skillet with cooking spray; heat over medium heat until hot. Add chicken. Cook and stir 3 minutes or until chicken is lightly browned and no longer pink in center.

2. Combine pineapple juice, peanut butter, oyster sauce and chili paste in small bowl until smooth. Place tortillas on baking sheets. Spread peanut butter mixture over tortillas. Divide chicken, carrot, green onions, pepper and cilantro evenly between each tortilla. Sprinkle with cheese. Bake 5 minutes or until tortillas are crisp and cheese is melted. Cut into wedges.

Makes 4 servings

Cook's Notes

Oyster sauce is a thick, brown, concentrated sauce made of ground oysters, soy sauce and brine. It imparts very little fish flavor to foods and is used as a seasoning to intensify other flavors.

Thai Chicken Pizza

Grilled Pizza

▌▌▌

2 loaves (1 pound each)
    frozen bread dough,
    thawed*
Olive oil
K.C. MASTERPIECE®
    Barbecue Sauce or pizza
    sauce
Seasonings: finely chopped
    garlic and fresh or dried
    herbs
Toppings: any combination
    of slivered ham, shredded
    barbecued chicken and
    grilled vegetables, such
    as thinly sliced
    mushrooms, zucchini,
    yellow squash, bell
    peppers, eggplant,
    pineapple chunks,
    tomatoes
Salt and black pepper
Cheese: any combination of
    shredded mozzarella,
    provolone, Monterey
    Jack, grated Parmesan or
    crumbled feta

*Substitute your favorite pizza crust recipe. Dough for 1 large pizza will make 4 individual ones.

Divide each loaf of dough into 4 balls. Roll on cornmeal-coated or lightly floured surface and pat out dough to ¼-inch thickness to make small circles. Brush each circle with oil.

Arrange hot **KINGSFORD®** briquets on one side of the grill. Oil hot grid to help prevent sticking. Vegetables, such as mushrooms, zucchini, yellow squash, bell peppers and eggplant need to be grilled until tender before using them as toppings. (See Note below.)

Place 4 circles directly above medium Kingsford® briquets. (The dough will not fall through the grid.) Grill circles, on uncovered grill, until dough starts to bubble in spots on the top and the bottom gets lightly browned. Turn over using tongs. Continue to grill until the other side is lightly browned, then move the crusts to the cool part of the grill.

Brush each crust lightly with barbecue sauce; top with garlic and herbs, then meat or vegetables. Season with salt and pepper, then top with cheese. Cover pizzas and grill, about 5 minutes until cheese melts, bottom of crust is crisp and pizza looks done. Repeat with remaining dough.
Makes 8 individual pizzas

Note: Vegetables such as mushrooms, zucchini, yellow squash, bell peppers and eggplant should be grilled before adding to pizza. If used raw, they will not have enough time to cook through. To grill, thread cut-up vegetables on skewers. Brush lightly with oil. Grill vegetables, on uncovered grill, over hot Kingsford® briquets, until tender, turning frequently. Or place piece of wire mesh on grid, such as the type used for screen doors, to keep vegetables from slipping through grid.

Ham & Pineapple Pizza: Brush crust lightly with K.C. Masterpiece® Barbecue Sauce and top with minced garlic, slivered ham, grilled bell peppers, pineapple chunks and shredded mozzarella or Monterey Jack cheese.

Veggie-Herb Pizza: Brush crust lightly with pizza sauce and top with finely chopped basil, minced garlic and grilled mushrooms, zucchini and green bell pepper. Sprinkle with grated Parmesan cheese.

Tomato-Feta Pizza: Top crust with minced garlic and crumbled dried herbs or minced fresh herbs, such as oregano, rosemary and basil. Top with chopped fresh tomato, slivered red onion and coarsely chopped olives. Sprinkle with grated Parmesan cheese and crumbled feta cheese.

Grilled Pizzas

SANDWICH EXPRESS

Monte Cristo Sandwiches

▌▌▌

⅓ cup **HELLMANN'S®** or **BEST FOODS®** Real or Light Mayonnaise or Low Fat Mayonnaise Dressing
¼ teaspoon ground nutmeg
⅛ teaspoon freshly ground pepper
12 slices white bread, crusts removed
6 slices Swiss cheese
6 slices cooked ham
6 slices cooked chicken
2 eggs
½ cup milk

1. In small bowl, combine mayonnaise, nutmeg and pepper; spread on one side of each bread slice.

2. Layer cheese, ham and chicken on 6 bread slices; top with remaining bread, mayonnaise sides down. Cut sandwiches diagonally into quarters.

3. In small bowl, beat together eggs and milk; dip sandwich quarters into egg mixture.

4. Cook on preheated greased griddle or in skillet, turning once, 4 to 5 minutes or until browned and heated through.
Makes 24 mini sandwiches

Eggplant & Pepper Cheese Sandwiches

▮ ▮ ▮

1 (8-ounce) eggplant, cut into 18 slices
Salt and black pepper, to taste
⅓ cup GREY POUPON® COUNTRY DIJON® Mustard
¼ cup olive oil
2 tablespoons red wine vinegar
¾ teaspoon dried oregano leaves
1 clove garlic, crushed
6 (4-inch) pieces French bread, cut in half
1 (7-ounce) jar roasted red peppers, cut into strips
1½ cups shredded mozzarella cheese (6 ounces)

Place eggplant slices on greased baking sheet, overlapping slightly. Sprinkle lightly with salt and pepper. Bake at 400°F for 10 to 12 minutes or until tender.

Blend mustard, oil, vinegar, oregano and garlic. Brush eggplant slices with ¼ cup mustard mixture; broil eggplant for 1 minute.

Brush cut sides of French bread with remaining mustard mixture. Layer 3 slices eggplant, a few red pepper strips and ¼ cup cheese on each bread bottom. Place on broiler pan with roll tops, cut-sides up; broil until cheese melts. Close sandwiches with bread tops and serve immediately; garnish as desired.

Makes 6 sandwiches

Cook's Nook

When purchasing eggplant, look for a firm eggplant that is heavy for its size, with a tight glossy, deeply-colored skin. The stem should be bright green. Dull skin and rust-colored spots are a sign of old age. Refrigerate unwashed eggplant in a plastic bag for up to 5 days.

Bistro Turkey Sandwiches

▌▌▌

¼ cup reduced-calorie
   mayonnaise
2 tablespoons finely chopped
   fresh basil
2 tablespoons chopped
   drained sun-dried
   tomatoes in oil
2 tablespoons finely chopped
   pitted kalamata olives
⅛ teaspoon red pepper flakes
1 loaf focaccia bread,
   quartered and split *or*
   8 slices sourdough bread
1 jar (7 ounces) roasted red
   bell peppers, rinsed and
   drained
4 romaine or red leaf lettuce
   leaves
2 packages (4 ounces each)
   HEBREW NATIONAL®
   Sliced Oven Roasted or
   Smoked Turkey Breast

Combine mayonnaise, basil,
sun-dried tomatoes, olives and
red pepper in small bowl; mix
well. Spread evenly over cut
sides of bread. Remove excess
liquid from roasted red bell
peppers with paper towels.
Layer roasted peppers, lettuce
and turkey breast between
bread slices.

Makes 4 servings

Amigo Pita Pocket Sandwiches

▌▌▌

1 pound ground turkey
1 can (7 ounces) whole
   kernel corn, drained
1 can (6 ounces) tomato
   paste
½ cup water
½ cup chopped green bell
   pepper
1 package (1.0 ounce)
   LAWRY'S® Taco Spices &
   Seasonings
8 pita breads
   Curly lettuce leaves
   Shredded Cheddar cheese

In large skillet, brown ground
turkey until no longer pink;
drain fat. Add corn, tomato
paste, water, bell pepper and
Taco Spices & Seasonings; mix
well. Bring to a boil over
medium-high heat; reduce heat
to low and cook, uncovered, 15
minutes. Cut off top quarter of
pita breads and open to form
pockets. Line each with lettuce
leaves. Spoon about ½ cup
filling into each pita bread and
top with cheese.

Makes 8 servings

Serving Suggestion: Serve with
vegetable sticks and fresh fruit.

Bistro Turkey Sandwich

French Dip Sandwiches

▮▮▮

½ cup A.1.® Original or A.1.®
   Bold & Spicy Steak
   Sauce, divided
1 tablespoon GREY POUPON®
   Dijon Mustard
4 steak rolls, split
   horizontally
8 ounces sliced cooked roast
   beef
1 (13¾-fluid ounce) can beef
   broth

In small bowl, blend ¼ cup steak sauce and mustard; spread mixture evenly on cut sides of roll tops. Arrange 2 ounces beef on each roll bottom; replace roll tops over beef. Slice sandwiches in half crosswise if desired. In small saucepan, heat broth and remaining ¼ cup steak sauce, stirring occasionally. Serve as a dipping sauce with sandwiches. Garnish as desired.

Makes 4 servings

French Dip Sandwich

Grilled Eggplant Sandwiches

▌▌▌

1 eggplant (about
    1¼ pounds)
Salt and black pepper
6 thin slices provolone
    cheese
6 thin slices deli-style ham or
    mortadella
  Fresh basil leaves
    (optional)
  Olive oil

Cut eggplant into 12 (⅜-inch-thick) rounds; sprinkle both sides with salt and pepper. Top each of 6 eggplant slices with slice of cheese, slice of meat (fold or tear to fit) and a few basil leaves, if desired. Cover with slice of eggplant. Brush one side with olive oil. Secure each sandwich with 2 or 3 toothpicks.

Oil hot grid to help prevent sticking. Grill eggplant, oil side down, on covered grill, over medium **KINGSFORD®** briquets, 15 to 20 minutes. Halfway through cooking time, brush top with oil, then turn and continue grilling until eggplant is tender when pierced. (When turning, position sandwiches so toothpicks extend down between spaces in grid.) If eggplant starts to char, move to cooler part of grill.

Let sandwiches cool about 5 minutes, then cut into halves or quarters, if desired. Serve warm or at room temperature.

Makes 6 sandwiches

Mediterranean Pita Sandwiches

▌▌▌

1 cup plain nonfat yogurt
1 tablespoon chopped fresh
    cilantro
2 cloves garlic, minced
1 teaspoon lemon juice
1 can (15 ounces) chick-
    peas, drained and rinsed
1 can (14 ounces) cooked
    artichoke hearts,
    drained, rinsed and
    coarsely chopped
1½ cups thinly sliced
    cucumbers, cut into
    halves
½ cup shredded carrot
½ cup chopped green onions
4 whole wheat pitas, cut into
    halves

1. Combine yogurt, cilantro, garlic and lemon juice in small bowl.

2. Combine chick-peas, artichoke hearts, cucumbers, carrot and green onions in medium bowl. Stir in yogurt mixture until well blended. Divide cucumber mixture among pita halves.

Makes 4 servings

Mustard-Glazed Chicken Sandwiches

█ █ █

½ cup honey-mustard
    barbecue sauce, divided
4 Kaiser rolls, split
4 boneless skinless chicken
    breast halves (1 pound)
4 slices Swiss cheese
4 leaves leaf lettuce
8 slices tomato

1. Spread about 1 teaspoon barbecue sauce on cut sides of each roll.

2. Pound chicken breast halves between 2 pieces of plastic wrap to ½-inch thickness with flat side of meat mallet or rolling pin. Spread remaining barbecue sauce over chicken.

3. Cook chicken in large nonstick skillet over medium-low heat 5 minutes per side or until no longer pink in center. Remove skillet from heat. Place cheese slices on chicken; let stand 3 minutes to melt.

4. Place lettuce leaves and tomato slices on roll bottoms; top with chicken and roll tops.

Makes 4 servings

Prep and Cook Time:
19 minutes

Veggie Club Sandwiches

█ █ █

¼ cup reduced-fat mayonnaise
1 clove garlic, minced
⅛ teaspoon dried marjoram
    leaves
⅛ teaspoon dried tarragon
    leaves
8 slices whole-grain bread
8 leaf lettuce leaves
1 large tomato, thinly sliced
1 small cucumber, thinly
    sliced
4 reduced-fat Cheddar cheese
    slices
1 medium red onion, thinly
    sliced and separated into
    rings
½ cup alfalfa sprouts

1. To prepare mayonnaise spread, combine mayonnaise, garlic, marjoram and tarragon in small bowl. Refrigerate until ready to use.

2. To assemble sandwiches, spread each of 4 bread slices with 1 tablespoon mayonnaise spread. Divide lettuce, tomato, cucumber, cheese, onion and sprouts among bread slices. Top with remaining bread. Cut sandwiches into halves and serve immediately.

Makes 4 sandwiches

Mustard-Glazed Chicken Sandwich

Mediterranean Chicken Salad Sandwiches

▮▮▮

4 boneless skinless chicken breast halves
1 teaspoon dried basil leaves
¼ teaspoon salt
¼ teaspoon black pepper
1 cup chopped cucumber
½ cup mayonnaise
¼ cup chopped roasted red pepper
¼ cup pitted black olive slices
¼ cup yogurt
¼ teaspoon garlic powder
6 Kaiser rolls, split
Additional mayonnaise
Lettuce leaves

Place chicken, ½ cup water, basil, salt and pepper in medium saucepan; bring to a boil. Reduce heat; simmer covered 10 to 12 minutes or until chicken is no longer pink in center. Remove chicken from saucepan; cool. Cut into ½-inch pieces.

Combine chicken, cucumber, mayonnaise, red pepper, olives, yogurt and garlic powder in medium bowl; toss to coat well.

Spread rolls with additional mayonnaise. Top with lettuce and chicken salad mixture.

Makes 6 servings

Philadelphia Cheese Steak Sandwiches

▮▮▮

2 cups sliced red or green bell peppers (about 2 medium)
1 small onion, thinly sliced
1 tablespoon vegetable oil
½ cup A.1.® Original or A.1.® Bold & Spicy Steak Sauce
1 teaspoon prepared horseradish
8 ounces thinly sliced beef sandwich steaks
4 ounces thinly sliced mozzarella cheese
4 long sandwich rolls, split

In medium saucepan, over medium heat, sauté pepper and onion slices in oil until tender. Stir in steak sauce and horseradish; keep warm.

In lightly greased medium skillet, over medium-high heat, cook sandwich steaks until done. Portion beef, pepper mixture and cheese on roll bottoms.

Broil sandwich bottoms 4 inches from heat source for 3 to 5 minutes or until cheese melts; replace tops. Serve immediately.

Makes 4 sandwiches

Philadelphia Cheese Steak Sandwich

Spicy Sesame Turkey Sandwich

▮▮▮

½ cup mayonnaise
1½ teaspoons LAWRY'S® Pinch
   of Herbs, divided
1½ teaspoons LAWRY'S® Lemon
   Pepper, divided
1 teaspoon sesame oil
1 teaspoon fresh lemon juice
4 or 5 turkey cutlets (about
   1¼ pounds)
½ cup all-purpose flour
2 tablespoons toasted
   sesame seeds
¼ to ½ teaspoon cayenne
   pepper
¼ cup milk
¼ cup vegetable oil
6 whole wheat buns, toasted
1 tomato, cut into 6 slices
6 sprigs watercress

In small bowl, combine mayonnaise, ½ teaspoon Pinch of Herbs, ½ teaspoon Lemon Pepper, sesame oil and lemon juice; cover. Refrigerate until ready to serve. Cut turkey into six equal portions. In large resealable plastic food storage bag, combine flour, sesame seeds, cayenne pepper, remaining Pinch of Herbs and remaining Lemon Pepper. Dip each turkey cutlet into milk. Add turkey, a few pieces at a time, to plastic bag; seal bag.

Shake until well coated. In large, heavy skillet, heat oil. Add turkey; cook over medium heat 5 to 8 minutes or until no longer pink in center, turning halfway through cooking time. Spread cut sides of buns with mayonnaise mixture. Top bottom half of each bun with turkey; cover with tomato, watercress and top half of roll.

Makes 6 servings

Serving Suggestion: Serve with coleslaw and juicy watermelon.

Cook's Notes

To toast sesame seeds, spread the seeds out in a small skillet. Shake the skillet over medium heat for 2 minutes or until the seeds begin to pop and turn golden.

Spicy Sesame Turkey Sandwich

DOUBLE-TIME

Grasshopper Pie

▪▪▪

2 cups graham cracker crumbs

**4 tablespoons unsweetened cocoa
powder**

¼ cup margarine, melted

**8 ounces nonfat cream cheese,
softened**

1 cup low-fat (1%) milk

**2 tablespoons green crème de
menthe liqueur**

**2 tablespoons white crème de
menthe liqueur**

1½ teaspoons vanilla

**1 container (4 ounces) frozen
whipped topping, thawed**

Spray 9-inch pie plate with nonstick
cooking spray. Combine cracker
crumbs, cocoa and margarine in
medium bowl. Press onto bottom
and up side of prepared pie plate.
Refrigerate. Beat cream cheese in
large bowl with electric mixer until
fluffy. Gradually beat in milk until
smooth. Stir in both liqueurs and
vanilla. Fold in whipped topping.
Refrigerate 20 minutes or until
chilled, but not set. Pour into chilled
crust. Freeze 4 hours or until set.

Makes 8 servings

DESSERTS

Apple, Caramel and Nut Roll-Ups

▮▮▮

½ cup chopped pecans
3 large Jonathan apples
1 tablespoon butter or margarine
1 teaspoon ground nutmeg
¼ teaspoon ground cinnamon
6 (8-inch) thin flour tortillas
¾ cup caramel sauce
Whipped cream

1. Preheat oven to 300°F. Spread pecans in shallow baking pan. Bake 20 to 30 minutes or until lightly browned; set aside.

2. While toasting pecans, peel, core and slice apples. Place in microwavable container. Top with butter, nutmeg and cinnamon. Microwave, covered, on HIGH, stirring once, 3 minutes or until tender; set aside. Place tortillas in plastic bag (do not seal). Microwave on HIGH 30 to 45 seconds or until heated through; set aside. Place caramel sauce in microwavable container. Microwave on HIGH 30 to 45 seconds or until hot.

3. Lay tortillas flat on work surface. Spoon ⅙ of the apples down center of each tortilla. Top with 1 tablespoon nuts and 1 tablespoon sauce. Fold one side tortilla over filling; roll up. Place on large serving platter or individual plates. Drizzle each crêpe with about 1 tablespoon sauce. Top with whipped cream and 1 teaspoon nuts.

Makes 6 servings

Prep and Cook Time:
20 minutes

Summer Fruits with Peanut Butter-Honey Dip

▮▮▮

⅓ cup smooth or chunky peanut butter
2 tablespoons milk
2 tablespoons honey
1 tablespoon apple juice or water
⅛ teaspoon ground cinnamon
2 cups melon balls, including cantaloupe and honeydew
1 peach or nectarine, pitted and cut into 8 wedges
1 banana, peeled and thickly sliced

1. Place peanut butter in small bowl; gradually stir in milk and honey until blended. Stir in apple juice and cinnamon until mixture is smooth. Transfer to large bowl.

2. Serve dip along with prepared fruits.

*Makes 4 servings
(about ½ cup dip)*

Apple, Caramel and Nut Roll-Up

Apple-Gingerbread Mini Cakes

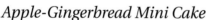

1 large Cortland or Jonathan apple, cored and quartered
1 package (14½ ounces) gingerbread cake and cookie mix
1 cup water
1 egg
 Powdered sugar

1. Lightly grease 10 (6- to 7-ounce) custard cups; set aside. Grate apple in food processor or with hand-held grater. Combine grated apple, cake mix, water and egg in medium bowl; stir until well blended. Spoon about ⅓ cup mix into each custard cup, filling cups half full.

2. Arrange 5 cups in microwave. Microwave on HIGH 2 minutes. Rotate cups ½ turn. Microwave 1 minute more or until cakes are springy when touched lightly and look a little moist on top. Cool on wire rack. Repeat with remaining cakes.

3. To unmold cakes, run a small knife around edge of custard cups to loosen cakes while still warm. Invert on cutting board and tap lightly until cake drops out. Place on plates. Dust with powdered sugar, using a design template, if desired. Serve warm or at room temperature.

Makes 10 cakes

Serving Suggestion: Serve with vanilla ice cream, whipped cream or crème anglaise.

Prep and Cook Time: 20 minutes

Apple-Gingerbread Mini Cake

Lemon Meringue Pie

▌▌▌

1 cup graham cracker crumbs
¼ cup powdered sugar
2 tablespoons margarine, melted
1 tablespoon water
1½ cups granulated sugar, divided
⅓ cup cornstarch
1½ cups hot water
¼ cup cholesterol-free egg substitute
1½ teaspoons grated lemon peel
½ cup fresh lemon juice
3 egg whites
½ teaspoon vanilla
¼ teaspoon cream of tartar

1. Preheat oven to 375°F. Combine graham cracker crumbs and powdered sugar in small bowl. Stir in margarine and water; mix until crumbs are moistened. Press crumb mixture onto bottom and up side of 9-inch pie plate. Bake 6 to 9 minutes or until edges are golden brown. Cool on wire rack. *Reduce oven temperature to 350°F.*

2. Combine ½ cup granulated sugar and cornstarch in medium saucepan over low heat. Gradually stir in hot water until smooth. Add egg substitute. Bring to a boil, stirring constantly with wire whisk. Boil 1 minute. Remove from heat; stir in lemon peel and lemon juice. Pour hot filling into cooled crust.

3. Beat egg whites, vanilla and cream of tartar in large bowl until soft peaks form. Gradually add remaining 1 cup granulated sugar, beating until stiff peaks form. Spread meringue over filling, sealing carefully to edge of crust.

4. Bake 12 to 15 minutes or until meringue is golden brown. Cool to room temperature before serving.
Makes 8 servings

CUTTING CORNERS

For ease in serving crumb crust pie, dip the pie plate just to the rim in hot water for 30 seconds to soften the crust slightly. Cut and serve.

Oreo® Cheesecake

▐▐▐

1 (20-ounce) package OREO®
 Chocolate Sandwich
 Cookies
⅓ cup margarine, melted
3 (8-ounce) packages cream
 cheese, softened
¾ cup sugar
4 eggs, at room temperature
1 cup dairy sour cream
1 teaspoon vanilla
 Whipped cream for garnish

Preheat oven to 350°F. Finely roll 30 cookies; coarsely chop 20 cookies. In medium bowl, combine finely rolled cookie crumbs and margarine. Press on bottom and 2 inches up side of 9-inch springform pan; set aside.

In large bowl with electric mixer at medium speed, beat cream cheese and sugar until creamy. Blend in eggs, sour cream and vanilla; fold in chopped cookies. Spread mixture into prepared crust. Bake at 350°F 60 minutes or until set.

Cool on wire rack at room temperature. Chill at least 4 hours. Halve remaining cookies; remove side of pan. To serve, garnish with whipped cream and cookie halves.

Makes 12 servings

Mocha Parfaits

▐▐▐

1½ tablespoons margarine
⅓ cup unsweetened cocoa
 powder
1 cup boiling water
½ cup sugar
1 tablespoon instant coffee
 granules
1 teaspoon vanilla
1 pint coffee-flavored nonfat
 frozen yogurt
12 whole coffee beans
 (optional)

1. Melt margarine in heavy saucepan over low heat. Add cocoa; cook and stir 3 minutes. Add boiling water, sugar and coffee; cook and stir until thickened. Remove from heat; stir in vanilla. Cool.

2. Place 2 tablespoons frozen yogurt in bottom of each of 4 parfait glasses. Top each with 1 tablespoon sauce. Top sauce with another 2 tablespoons frozen yogurt; top frozen yogurt with 2 tablespoons sauce. Repeat layering twice more. Top each parfait with 3 coffee beans, if desired.

Makes 4 servings

Sundae Shortcakes

▐ ▌ ▌

1 cup sugar
⅓ cup thawed frozen orange
  juice concentrate
3 tablespoons butter or
  margarine
1 can (17.3 ounces)
  refrigerated buttermilk
  biscuits
1 pint frozen vanilla or fruit-
  flavored yogurt or vanilla
  ice cream
3 cups fresh or frozen
  blackberries, thawed
Frozen whipped topping

1. Combine sugar, orange juice concentrate, ⅓ cup water and butter in small saucepan. Bring to a boil over medium-high heat, stirring constantly until sugar is melted. Boil gently, uncovered, 5 minutes.

2. Prepare biscuits according to package directions. Pierce 4 biscuits all over with skewer. Spoon ¼ of sugar mixture over 4 biscuits. Reserve remaining biscuits for another use. Let stand 1 minute.

3. Split biscuits; place bottom halves on serving plates. Spoon yogurt evenly over bottoms; top with blackberries. Drizzle with remaining sugar mixture; top with biscuit tops.

Makes 4 servings

Serving Suggestion: Serve with frozen whipped topping.

Prep and Cook Time:
30 minutes

Magic Dip

▐ ▌ ▌

1 package (8 ounces)
  PHILADELPHIA BRAND®
  Cream Cheese, softened
1 cup BAKER'S® Semi-Sweet
  Real Chocolate Chips
½ cup BAKER'S® ANGEL
  FLAKE® Coconut, toasted
½ cup chopped peanuts

SPREAD cream cheese on bottom of 9-inch microwavable pie plate or quiche dish.

TOP with remaining ingredients.

MICROWAVE on MEDIUM (50% power) 3 to 4 minutes or until warm. Serve with graham crackers. Garnish, if desired.
Makes 6 to 8 servings

Prep Time: 5 minutes
Microwave Time: 4 minutes

Cherry Cheesecake Squares

▊▊▊

2 cups graham cracker
    crumbs
¼ cup sugar
¼ cup (½ stick) butter or
    margarine, melted
3 packages (8 ounces each)
    PHILADELPHIA BRAND®
    Cream Cheese, softened
¾ cup sugar
1 teaspoon vanilla
2 eggs
1 can (20 ounces) cherry pie
    filling

MIX crumbs, ¼ cup sugar and butter. Press into 13×9-inch baking pan. Bake at 325°F for 10 minutes.

MIX cream cheese, ¾ cup sugar and vanilla with electric mixer on medium speed until well blended. Add eggs; mix just until blended. Pour over crust.

BAKE at 325°F for 35 minutes or until center is almost set. Cool. Refrigerate 3 hours or overnight. Top with pie filling. Cut into squares.

Makes 18 servings

Prep Time: 20 minutes plus refrigerating
Bake Time: 35 minutes

Caramelized Peaches & Cream

▊▊▊

2 pounds sliced peeled
    unsweetened peaches or
    thawed and well-drained
    frozen peaches
2 tablespoons bourbon
¾ cup reduced-fat sour cream
½ teaspoon ground cinnamon
¼ teaspoon ground nutmeg
¾ cup packed light brown
    sugar
8 slices (1½ ounces each)
    angel food cake

1. Toss peaches with bourbon in shallow ovenproof 1½-quart casserole or 11×7-inch glass baking dish. Press down into even layer.

2. Combine sour cream, cinnamon and nutmeg in small bowl; mix well. Spoon mixture evenly over peaches. (May be covered and refrigerated up to 2 hours before cooking time.)

3. Preheat broiler. Sprinkle brown sugar evenly over sour cream mixture to cover. Broil 4 to 5 inches from heat, 3 to 5 minutes or until brown sugar is melted and bubbly. (Watch closely after 3 minutes so that sugar does not burn.)

4. Spoon immediately over angel food cake.

Makes 8 servings

Blueberry Dream Fritters

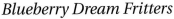

Vegetable oil
½ cup whipping cream
1 egg
1 teaspoon vanilla
1 cup self-rising flour
⅓ cup self-rising cornmeal
⅓ cup sugar
1½ cups fresh blueberries

1. Heat 2 inches oil in large heavy skillet to 375°F on deep-fat thermometer.

2. Meanwhile, stir together cream, egg and vanilla.

3. Combine flour, cornmeal and sugar in large bowl. Stir in cream mixture just until moistened. Fold in blueberries.

4. Carefully drop batter by heaping tablespoonfuls into hot oil. Fry until golden brown, turning once. Drain well on paper towels.

Makes 12 fritters

Serving Suggestion: Sprinkle fritters with powdered sugar.

Prep and Cook Time:
19 minutes

Blueberry Dream Fritters

Strawberry Margarita Pie

▌▌▌

3 tablespoons margarine
2 tablespoons honey
1½ cups crushed pretzels
3 cups low-fat sugar-free
    strawberry frozen yogurt,
    softened
1½ cups light nondairy whipped
    topping, thawed
2 teaspoons grated lime peel,
    divided
1 package (16 ounces)
    strawberries in syrup,
    thawed
1 tablespoon lime juice
1 tablespoon tequila
    (optional)

1. Combine margarine and honey in medium microwavable bowl. Microwave on HIGH 30 seconds or until smooth when stirred. Add pretzels; stir until evenly coated. Press into bottom and side of 9-inch pie plate; freeze 30 minutes or until firm.

2. Combine frozen yogurt, whipped topping and 1 teaspoon lime peel in medium bowl; gently fold with rubber spatula or wire whisk. Spoon into pie plate. Freeze 2 hours or until firm.

3. Combine strawberries, lime juice and remaining 1 teaspoon peel in small bowl; stir to blend.

4. Cut pie into 8 portions; serve with strawberry mixture. Add tequila to strawberry mixture just before serving, if desired.

Makes 8 servings

Mango Coconut Tropical Freeze

▌▌▌

1 jar (26 ounces) refrigerated
    mango slices, drained (or
    the flesh of 3 ripe
    mangoes, peeled and cut
    to equal about 3⅓ cups)
½ cup canned coconut cream
1 tablespoon lime juice
⅓ cup toasted chopped
    pecans

1. Place mango, coconut cream and lime juice in food processor; process 1 to 2 minutes or until smooth.

2. Spoon into small dessert cups or custard cups. Top with pecans. Place cups on pie plate, cover tightly. Freeze 8 hours or overnight. Remove from freezer and allow to thaw slightly before serving. Serve immediately.

Makes 4 servings

Make-Ahead Time: up to 1 day before serving
Final Prep Time: about 30 minutes

Strawberry Margarita Pie

ACKNOWLEDGMENTS

The publishers would like to thank the companies and organizations listed below for the use of their recipes and photographs in this publication.

A.1.® Steak Sauce

Bestfoods

Birds Eye®

Bob Evans®

Butterball® Turkey Company

Del Monte Corporation

Dole Food Company, Inc.

Egg Beaters® Healthy Real Egg Substitute

GREY POUPON® Mustard

Hebrew National®

Hillshire Farm®

The HV Company

Kikkoman International Inc.

The Kingsford Products Company

Kraft Foods, Inc.

Lawry's® Foods, Inc.

Lipton®

McIlhenny Company (TABASCO® Pepper Sauce)

National Pork Producers Council

OREO® Cookies

The Procter & Gamble Company

Reckitt & Colman Inc.

The J.M. Smucker Company

StarKist® Seafood Company

Veg-All®

Wisconsin Milk Marketing Board

INDEX